"Okay, but first we'll have to churn

the milk and hang out the laundry …

And then we'll need to do some weeding.   *Maybe we'll go after that.*

Oh, but hang on, we have lots of other chores to do too.

Maybe some other time!"

"Oh, but you promised that we'd go on a picnic … "

NOTE: At Barbizon, where Millet lived, farming wheat would actually begin with sowing seeds in fall and end with harvesting the wheat in summer. However, in *Let's Go on a Picnic*, for convenience, the story has the seeds being sowed in spring and harvested in fall.

big & SMALL

Original Korean text by Seon-hak Jo
Illustrations by Ji-won Baek
Korean edition © Aram Publishing

This English edition published by big & SMALL in 2017
by arrangement with Aram Publishing
English text edited by Scott Forbes
English edition © big & SMALL 2017

Distributed in the United States and Canada by
Lerner Publishing Group, Inc.
241 First Avenue North
Minneapolis, MN 55401 U.S.A.
www.lernerbooks.com

ISBN: 978-1-925235-27-2

Printed in Korea

Let's go on a Picnic!

THE ART OF MILLET

Written by Seon-hak Jo
Illustrated by Ji-won Baek
Edited by Scott Forbes

Spring (1868–73), Musée d'Orsay, Paris, France

6

Spring had arrived, and little Marie was excited. "Mom, let's go on a picnic with Dad and Baby Julie!" she said.

"Sure," replied her mother. "As soon as we finish sowing these seeds, we'll go."

7

"Dad," asked Marie, "when will you start sowing seeds?"

"Not for a while," said her father. "First we have to turn over the soil to make it nice and soft. Otherwise, if the ground is too hard, the seeds won't sprout."

"But that's going to take days and days!" said Marie.

"That's about right," replied her father.

Man with a Hoe (1860–62), Getty Museum, Los Angeles, USA

The Sower (1850),
Museum of Fine Arts,
Boston, USA

"Dad, have you finished sowing the seeds yet?" asked Marie.

"No," replied her father, "there's still a long way to go. After I sow these seeds in the field, I need to cover them with soft soil so that they won't blow away when the wind gets up."

"You need to cover this whole field?!" said Marie. "Then I guess I'll have to wait another few days."

11

"Mom, spring will soon be over.
When are we going on a picnic?"
asked Marie once more.

"Look outside, dear," said her mother.
"Can't you see that it's raining?
We'll have to wait for a nicer day."

13

Churning Butter (1866–68), Musée d'Orsay, Paris, France

14

"Mom," said Marie, "let's go to that shady valley for a picnic. If Dad's too busy, maybe you and I can go with Baby Julie."

"Well," replied her mother, "maybe after I churn the milk, do the laundry, and dig the weeds out of the garden, we can go on a picnic with Dad."

15

"Dad, Mom has churned the milk, done the laundry, and weeded the garden. And the wheat you planted has already started to grow. Surely now we can go on a picnic?" pleaded Marie.

"Not today, I'm afraid," said her dad.
"I need to chop the firewood and
separate the seeds."

17

"Mom, look. I've grown taller
and Julie is walking now.
Please, can we go on an
outing together?" begged Marie.

"Okay," said her mom. "Why don't
you take Julie up to Peter's house
on the hill. I hear his cow is about
to give birth to a calf."

Peasants Bringing Home a Calf Born in the Fields (1864),
Art Institute of Chicago,
Chicago, USA

But Peter's cow had already given birth to its calf in the fields. When Marie and Julie arrived, they saw Peter and his farmhands carrying the calf into the courtyard.

Marie wished her mom and dad could have seen the newborn calf too.

"When the harvest finishes," she said to little Julie, "we'll all come back to Peter's house together."

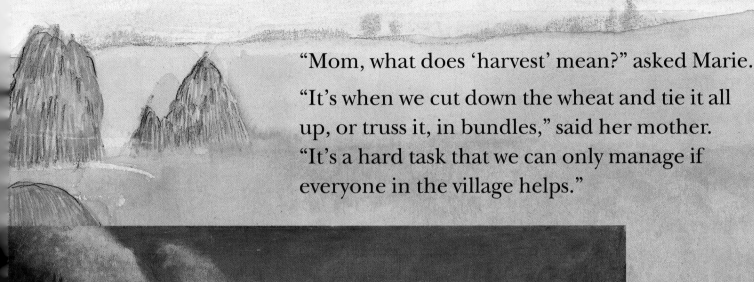

"Mom, what does 'harvest' mean?" asked Marie.

"It's when we cut down the wheat and tie it all up, or truss it, in bundles," said her mother. "It's a hard task that we can only manage if everyone in the village helps."

The Hay Trussers (1850–51), Musée du Louvre, Paris, France

23

The Gleaners (1857), Musée d'Orsay, Paris, France

"Mom, when will you be finished harvesting?" asked Marie. "I'm hungry and bored, and Julie has fallen asleep. Can we go home now?"

"Just wait a little longer, dear," her mom said. "We have to pick up all the grains that have fallen on the ground. We can't let them go to waste, can we?"

25

"Come over here, child," said Marie's mother. "Now the harvest has finished, we should pray."

"Should we pray for more wheat?" asked Marie.

"No, the soil can only give us the wheat from the seeds we plant," replied her mother.

"Should we pray for the work to be easier?" asked Marie.

"No, to be rewarded in life you have to work hard."

"So what should we pray for?" said Marie.

"Just give thanks for all we have."

The Angelus (1857–59), Musée d'Orsay, Paris, France

27

"Yippee!" shouted Marie.
"My wish has come true!
Mom and Dad and Julie
and I are finally setting
off. At last, we're
going on a picnic!"

28

Biography of Jean-François Millet

Noble lives revealed

Jean-François Millet was born in 1814, in a small village called Gruchy, in the region of Normandy, in northwestern France. Millet was a very bright boy and the local priests helped him get a good education. They recognized his artistic talent and sent him to the port of Cherbourg to study with professional artists. Then, when he was in his early twenties, Millet moved to Paris to study at art school. However, he didn't enjoy it much and spent most of his time in the Louvre Museum copying famous works of art by painters such as Michelangelo, Nicolas Poussin, and Honoré Daumier.

Leaving for Barbizon

In 1848 there was a major uprising in Paris, followed by an outbreak of a deadly disease, cholera. To escape these troubles, Millet and his family moved to the village of Barbizon, in the countryside outside Paris. As Millet observed the local farmers working in the fields and raising crops each year, he was deeply moved. Although the farmers were poor, Millet felt they led noble lives, living in harmony with nature. From then on the peasants became the main subject of his art, and he would end up living in Barbizon for the rest of his life.

Man wth a Hoe (1860–62), Getty Museum, Los Angeles, USA
Many people thought the man in this painting was very ugly. But Millet pointed out that it was simply a realistic portrait of a hard-working peasant.

The Hay Trussers (1850–51) Musée du Louvre, Paris, France
This painting shows farmers rolling the hay around a stick to form a tight bundle. This is called trussing the hay.

1814
Born in Gruchy, France, on October 4

1833
Learns painting from teachers in Cherbourg

1837
Attends art school in Paris and studies famous paintings in the Louvre Museum

1841
Marries Pauline-Virginie Ono

1844
Paintings rejected by major art competition in Paris; returns to Cherbourg

1845
Pauline dies after a short illness

An unfamiliar world

For most of the wealthy people in Paris who enjoyed and bought paintings, the lifestyle of poor farmers was not a proper subject for art. They could not understand why Millet kept painting such scenes. But gradually they came to see that the paintings were not only beautiful but showed deep respect for the farmers and their hard work. And many of them began to understand the farmers better as a result of looking at Millet's paintings.

The Gleaners (1857), Musée d'Orsay, Paris, France

Spring (1868–73), Musée d'Orsay, Paris, France
This is a painting of the scenery around Barbizon. It shows the sky clearing after a storm to reveal a rainbow, but it also represents the happy arrival of spring after the hardships of winter.

Churning Butter (1866–68), Musée d'Orsay, Paris, France
This woman is churning up milk to make butter. This was a regular task for most farmers' wives.

1849
Moves to Barbizon with Catherine Lemaire

1850
Decides to devote himself to painting the local farmers

1857
Paints *The Gleaners*, one of his best-known works

1860s
People begin to admire and respect Millet's works

1868
Awarded the Legion of Honor by the French Government

1875
Dies on January 20

The stories behind *The Angelus*

The Millet painting that perhaps captures the lives of the poor Barbizon farmers most movingly is *The Angelus*. It shows a farmer and his wife standing in a field, praying. They are wearing old, ragged clothes and their simple tools are scattered around them. There is no one else nearby, but in the distance you can see a village and its church. The title of the painting is the name of a traditional prayer, recited to give thanks to God and remember people who have passed away.

In Millet's time, most farmers rented their houses and fields from rich landowners. When they harvested their crops, they had to hand them over to the landowner and in return were paid only a small wage. So they worked very hard to farm the land and received little in return. Their lives were hard and they usually remained poor. *The Angelus* conveys a keen sense of their poverty and the hard work they had to do, but also of their strong religious faith.

Winning fame

In 1859, Millet entered *The Angelus* into an art competition. It received a poor response from the judges. They made fun of it and said the two figures looked like scarecrows wearing rags. But by the 1880s *The Angelus* had become a hugely popular painting and the famous Louvre Museum in Paris tried to buy it for its collection. *The Angelus* also had a powerful influence on other painters. It showed them how a realistic, everyday scene could be beautiful and move people.

The Angelus (1857–59), Musée d'Orsay, Paris, France

The Sower (1850), Museum of Fine Arts, Boston, USA

A daily ritual

Millet may have seen farmers around Barbizon stop work to pray, but he also said that it was something that he himself had done as a child when he was with his grandmother. Whenever she heard the local church bells ringing, she would make Millet and his siblings stop what they were doing and recite the Angelus. So with this painting Millet was remembering part of his own life as well as showing the hard lives of the Barbizon farmers.

Intriguing other artists

Many later painters were fascinated by *The Angelus*, including the famous Dutch painter Vincent van Gogh (1853–90). Van Gogh was also interested in and painted poor farmers, and he was impressed by the warm and sympathetic way in which Millet had portrayed their lives. Van Gogh even made copies of a number of Millet paintings.

Another artist who was fascinated by Millet's work, and *The Angelus* in particular, was Salvador Dalí, a famous Spanish surrealist painter of the 20th century. After studying *The Angelus* for some time, he began to wonder why a painter as skilled as Millet had painted the vegetable basket in the foreground so roughly. He wondered if Millet had originally started painting something else and had then changed his mind and painted over it. In response to Dalí's questions, a museum decided to have the painting X-rayed. Underneath the vegetable basket there was a rather strange shape. It wasn't clear what it was. But Dalí claimed that the shape was a child's tomb and that the poor farmers had just buried and were praying for their lost child. Other scholars, however, who have studied Millet's paintings for years, have disagreed with Dalí, and we can't be sure if his theory is true.

Vincent van Gogh, *The Sower* (1889), Niarchos Collection, Zurich, Switzerland

"Thank goodness! No more gathering up grains for us.

We're going to have a wonderful day out!"